20th Century
PERSPECTIVES

The Persian Gulf War

Karen Price Hossell

Heinemann Library
Chicago, Illinois

Customer Service 888-454-2279
Visit our website at www.heinemannlibrary.com

Designed by Heinemann Library
Maps by John Fleck
Photo research by Bill Broyles
Originated by QueNet
Printed and bound in the United States by Lake Book Manufacturing, Inc.

07 06 05 04
10 9 8 7 6 5 4 3 2

Library of Congress Cataloging-in-Publication Data
Price Hossell, Karen, 1957–
  The Persian Gulf War / Karen Price Hossell.
    p. cm. -- (20th-century perspectives)
Includes bibliographical references and index.
  ISBN 1-4034-1143-3 (hardcover) ISBN 1-4034-3856-0 (paperback)
  1. Persian Gulf War, 1991--Juvenile literature. I. Title. II. Series.

DS79.723 .P75 2003
956.7044'2--dc21

Acknowledgments
The publisher is grateful to the following for permission to reproduce copyright material:
p. 5 Bush Presidential Library; p. 6 Erick Bonnier/Gamma Presse; p. 7 Jassim Mohammed/AP Wide World; p. 8 Thomas Hartwell/TimePix; pp. 9, 28 Bettmann/Corbis; p. 10 Sipa Press; p. 11 Najlah Feanny/Corbis SABA; p. 12 Alain Norgues/Corbis SYGMA; p. 13 Robert Azzi/Woodfin Camp & Associates; p. 14 J. A. Giorano/Corbis SABA; pp. 15, 41 Peter Turnley/Corbis; pp. 16, 19, 26 Corbis; p. 17 Ferry Stephen/Gamma Presse; pp. 18, 21, 22, 29, 37, 38 Department of Defense; p. 20 Ron Edmonds/AP Wide World Photo; p. 23 Moshe Shai/Corbis; p. 24 Van Der Stockt Laurent/Gamma Presse; p. 25 Saulnier Didier/Gamma Presse; p. 27 Eric Bouvet/Gamma Presse; p. 30 CNN International Sales LTD/G/Gamma Presse; p. 31 Terry Ashe/TimePix; pp. 32, 33 Joseph Sohm/ChromoSohm, Inc./Corbis; p. 34 Steve Bent/Katz/Woodfin Camp & Associates; p. 35 Barry Iverson/Woodfin Camp & Associates; p. 36 Lauren Rebours/AP Wide World Photo; p. 39 Steve McCurry/Magnum; p. 40 Karim Sahib/AFP/Corbis; p. 42 Faleh Kheiber/Reuters/Corbis; p. 43 Reuters/Corbis

Cover photograph by Peter Turnley/Corbis

Special thanks to Colonel Guy LoFaro, United States Army, FORSCOM, for his comments in the preparation of this book.

Some words are shown in bold, **like this.** You can find out what they mean by looking in the glossary.

Contents

Background

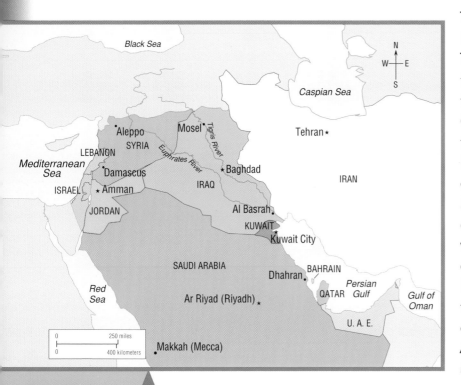

The Middle East has long been a region of conflict. The primary reason is that the area has been home to both Arabs and Jews. Conflicts between these two groups arise not only because of religious differences, but also because of disagreements over landownership. And while the primary disputes in the Middle East are between these two groups, there is also disagreement between Arab countries over borders.

This map shows Iraq, Kuwait, and Saudi Arabia. The Iraqi Army invaded Kuwait in 1990, and many military experts believed that Saudi Arabia was its next target.

The creation of Israel

Until World War I, the powerful **Ottoman Empire** had control of most of the region. After the war, however, the empire dissolved, and its lands were divided between several countries, including Great Britain. During World War II, many Jews fled to Palestine in the Middle East to escape the **Nazi regime**, which persecuted them. After the war, Britain gave a large section of Palestine to the Jews so they could establish their own state, called Israel. The Arabs felt betrayed—they had fought alongside the British in World War II and now felt that their land was being torn from them by Britain. Hostilities intensified between Arabs and Jews during that time, and have remained intense since then.

Oil

In the 1900s, another factor arose that turned the attention of many powerful countries toward the Middle East. In 1908, oil was discovered in Iran, and in 1927, it was discovered in Iraq. The United States produced oil during that time. It produced enough that it had little need for foreign oil.

That need changed by the middle of the century. Billions of barrels of U.S. oil were used by the **Allied** troops in World War II, and the United States began to worry that its oil supply was being used up. It looked to the Persian Gulf region of the Middle East to find more oil and gained access to oil deposits in Kuwait and Saudi Arabia. By the early 1970s, the United States depended on the Middle East for one-third of its oil. Because oil was in such great demand, the oil-producing countries in that area raised prices. But by the late 1980s, enough oil had been found elsewhere to meet the demand, so oil prices went down.

Troubles in Iraq

While leaders of Middle Eastern countries were not happy to see oil prices lowered, perhaps the most unhappy was Saddam Hussein, the leader of Iraq. His country had finished a long, eight-year war with Iran in 1988. To fight the war, Iraq had borrowed billions of dollars from other countries. Hussein planned to use profits from selling Iraqi oil to pay back the loans, but his plans were hindered when prices went down. One country in particular, Kuwait, was demanding that Iraq begin repaying its loan. Hussein believed that Kuwait should forgive the loan. He believed it was the sacrifice of his soldiers that had kept Iran from overrunning not only Iraq, but Kuwait as well.

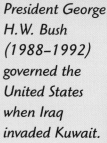

President George H.W. Bush (1988–1992) governed the United States when Iraq invaded Kuwait.

Iraq invades Kuwait

For these and other reasons, on August 2, 1990, the Iraqi army invaded Kuwait, and Hussein proclaimed that it was now Iraq's 19th province. With the takeover of oil-rich Kuwait, Hussein now controlled about twenty percent—one-fifth—of the world's oil supply.

The world, especially the United States, took notice of the invasion. Over the next few months, world leaders attempted to persuade Iraq to withdraw from Kuwait and gave it a deadline to do so. When the deadline passed, the Iraqis remained in Kuwait, and what is known as the Persian Gulf War began. The war was quick. When it ended, Iraq and its army were devastated, thousands of Iraqis were dead, and Kuwait was liberated.

The Middle East

Iraqi metal workers creating useful and decorative items. The Gulf War disrupted life in Iraq, and many of its people suffered greatly.

Until oil was discovered there in the 1900s, the primary interest in the Middle East by other governments was that it provided a route to Asia. Without the cooperation or control of countries in the Middle East, nations such as Great Britain would have to sail south around the tip of Africa, then north, in order to reach their Asian colonies. The Suez Canal and other parts of the Middle East provided quicker and easier access to the British colony of India and other regions.

A homeland

To the people whose ancestors had lived there for centuries, though, the Middle East was a homeland. In fact, some of the earliest known civilizations in the world developed in the Middle East. Occupation and leadership of these lands has changed hands many times over the centuries. The area has often been one of unrest as warring groups united by family, religious, or geographical ties competed for control.

Iraq

Iraq is known as the Cradle of Civilization because it was home to one of the earliest known civilizations, the Sumerians. They settled in the fertile region between the Tigris and Euphrates Rivers and cultivated the land for crops. Control of the area changed hands many times over the years, and, in the 1600s, the Turks took over and made the region part of their **Ottoman Empire.** They ruled the land until World War I, when their empire collapsed.

After the Ottoman Empire's fall, the British, hoping to find oil, took control of Baghdad and placed what is now Iraq under its rule. In 1921, British leaders in charge of the area met in Egypt and drew boundaries. While under Ottoman rule the region had consisted of three separate provinces. But the British combined all of the diverse populations into one country. They named the country *Iraq*, an Arab word that means the *well-rooted country.*

One year later, the British changed the borders. Saddam Hussein would later claim the changed borders as a reason for invading Kuwait. He saw the border as invalid and declared that Kuwait should be part of Iraq.

Eventually, the British government made Iraq an independent state, to be ruled as a kingdom. Iraq became fully independent in 1932. It was ruled by kings until 1958, when the **Ba'ath party** took over, killing most members of the ruling family in the process. In 1979, Saddam Hussein became president of Iraq.

Kuwait

Today, Kuwait is a tiny country, but unlike Iraq, it has a long coastline along the Persian Gulf. In the late 1800s, the Kuwaiti government, worried that the Turks wanted to make Kuwait part of the Ottoman Empire, looked to Great Britain for help. In 1899, Kuwait and Britain signed a **treaty**, and Kuwait became an independent country under British protection.

In searing temperatures, Iraqis work at an oil pumping station, which is a main fixture in both Iraq and Kuwait.

Oil was discovered in Kuwait in 1938, but World War II distracted the country from producing and exporting it. Oil export began in 1946, and by the 1950s, Kuwait was becoming a wealthy nation. In 1961, Kuwait's relationship with Britain changed when the 1899 treaty was replaced by a Treaty of Friendship, and Kuwait became independent of Britain. Today, Kuwait is ruled by the Al-Sabah family.

Saddam Hussein

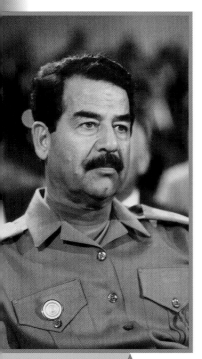

Saddam Hussein was born into a poor family in 1937. At ten years old, Saddam asked his parents to send him to school so he could learn to read and write, but they refused. Determined to achieve his goal, he ran away one night and went to live with his Uncle Kairallah. Kairallah became like a father to Hussein and influenced the boy's political beliefs, teaching Hussein to dislike non-Arabs.

In 1957, Saddam Hussein joined the **Ba'ath party,** an Arab political party with branches in several Arab countries. The party's primary goal is to unite all Arabs into one nation. Party members believe that the Arab world has been continually oppressed by various nations.

In 1959, Hussein and other Ba'ath party members tried to assassinate the leader of Iraq, Abdul Karim Kassem, with the goal of bringing the country under Ba'ath rule. Hussein was charged with the attempted assassination and sentenced to death. But he escaped from prison and fled to Syria and then Egypt. He returned to Iraq in 1963 and was eventually named the leader of the Ba'ath party.

Iraq's president, Saddam Hussein, rose from humble beginnings to hold the most powerful office in the country.

With the support of the Iraqi army, Hussein helped the Ba'ath party overthrow Iraq's government in 1968. The new government immediately conducted **purges,** by executing or imprisoning hundreds of Iraqis who disagreed with the new **regime.** At the time, Hussein was second in command in the Ba'ath party, or vice-president of Iraq.

In 1979, Saddam Hussein was named chairman of the Ba'ath party and president of Iraq. One of his first acts as president was to execute many senior officials in the government. In addition, he used a newly-formed secret police force to purge the army of any members he thought were disloyal to his government.

The Iran-Iraq War

Iraq's war with Iran was based on long-standing disputes over borders and the Shatt al-Arab waterway. But hostilities between the two countries were intensified by their religious differences. Both countries are **Muslim,** which means they follow the religion of **Islam,** but their leaders at that time were from two different branches of the religion. Iran's rulers are primarily **Shi'ite** Muslim. Iraq's were mainly Sunni

Iraqi soldiers fight in the Iranian desert during the Iran-Iraq War. The economic cost of the war was high. Iraq owed over $75 billion dollars to other countries, including Kuwait.

Muslim. Most Iraqi people are Shi'ites, however. Sunnis make up the majority—about 85 percent—of the world's Muslims. The remaining Muslims are Shi'ites.

In the 1970s, many clashes occurred on the border of Iran and Iraq. In September 1980, Iraq invaded Iran, and the Iran-Iraq War officially began. When the war ended in 1988, about one million Iranians and Iraqis were dead.

A rule of fear

The regime of Saddam Hussein was based on fear. To keep his power, Hussein did away with anyone who got in his way. Few around him dared question his actions.

During his presidency, Saddam Hussein committed crimes against the people of Iraq. In the late 1980s, he used poison gas against the **Kurds,** who live in northern Iraq. When he found out that the Kurds supported Iran in the Iran-Iraq War, he ordered **chemical weapons** to be dropped from the air onto the Kurdish village of Halabja. About 5,000 people were killed in that attack.

Hussein's goal

Saddam Hussein's goal of uniting the entire Arab world would have given him power not only in the Persian Gulf but also in a large percentage of the world's known oil reserves. A regime with that much control over the world's oil reserves could influence the world's economy by manipulating the price of oil. It was because of the world's dependence on oil—along with other more **humanitarian** reasons—that the United States and other countries were compelled to confront Saddam Hussein in the Persian Gulf War.

An Iraqi officer speaks

On March 2, 1991, a Marine intelligence specialist interviewed a captured Iraqi officer. When asked what he thought of Saddam Hussein, the officer replied:

We are very afraid of this man. Even now that I am talking to you, an American, you will notice that by habit, I will lower my voice when I want to say his name. He has spies everywhere. If he knows that I say bad things about him to you, he will kill my wife, my children, and my parents in Iraq.... Saddam Hussein is crazy and there can never be peace while he is alive.... Our people are not educated because they must serve in the army. There is no money for food, education, health care—just for war. What is the reason for this?

Lead-Up to War

The actions of Saddam Hussein after the Iran-Iraq War, combined with the reactions of other countries involved in the Middle East, led to conflicts that seemed to be leading to another war.

Beginning in July 1990, thousands of Iraqi troops gathered on the Iraq–Kuwait border.

Conflict over oil

After the Iran-Iraq War ended in 1988, the Kuwaiti government wanted Iraq to start paying back its $17 billion loan. The Iraqi government countered this request by accusing Kuwait of overproducing oil, which resulted in lower oil prices. Iraq also claimed that Kuwait had been stealing its oil. Hussein was convinced that the Kuwaitis were drilling diagonally from their portion of the Rumalia oil field into Iraqi-owned oil reserves. Eventually, Kuwait admitted that it was stealing oil from the Iraqi side of the border. It insisted, however, that it was only doing so to get back the money Iraq owed, and that the stolen oil was considered to be a down payment on the debt.

Border conflict

Hussein was also concerned that Kuwait was trying to expand into Iraq. Kuwait, he believed, should really be a part of Iraq—not the other way around. Decades earlier, the British government had given Saudi Arabia land that was once part of Kuwait. Hussein and others in Iraq believed that land should have instead gone to Iraq.

Hussein also felt that part of the reason Kuwait had lent Iraq money was that it feared the **Islamic fundamentalist** government of Iran. Iraq had spent eight years fighting the mutual enemy of much of the Arab world. Instead of being grateful for its sacrifice and excusing the debt, Kuwait was asking Iraq to pay it.

If Iraq was going to invade Kuwait, the sooner it did so, the better. Thanks to the loans it had received during the war, the Iraqi army was strong and fit, numbering about one million soldiers. Iraq had thousands of tanks and other armored vehicles and a stockpile of bombs and missiles. The Kuwaiti army, on the other hand, was weak. It would not be able to withstand an invasion by Iraq.

Ambassador meets with Hussein

Saddam Hussein needed to find out how the United States would react if he invaded Kuwait. He summoned the U.S. **ambassador** to Iraq, April Glaspie, to his office on July 25, 1991. There, he blamed the drop in the price of oil for an "economic war" against Iraq. He also stated that Iraq wanted to exist without interference from the United States.

At the meeting, Ambassador Glaspie told Hussein that the United States had "no opinion" about the border conflict between Iraq and Kuwait. Then she asked him to explain what he intended to do with the troops that were gathering at the Kuwaiti border. Hussein did not directly answer the question, but he did explain that he believed the Kuwaiti aid given to Iraq during the Iran-Iraq War should not be regarded as debt, because Iraq had defended Kuwait against Iran. He then asked the ambassador what President George H. W. Bush, who was the U.S. president at the time, would do if he were in the same situation.

After the meeting, Glaspie stated that it appeared that Iraq was not planning to invade Kuwait. She did caution, though, that if such an invasion took place, Kuwait would not be able to withstand it. Hussein most likely came away from the meeting believing that the United States would not become involved if Iraq invaded Kuwait. The **superpower** had not interfered in the Iran-Iraq War. Besides, he knew that the idea of any war was not a popular one in the United States. Many Americans had not supported the **Vietnam War**, which ended in 1975, and they did not want to become involved in another situation like that one.

An American man changes the price of gasoline to reflect the changing price of oil. Oil prices continually fluctuate based on supply, demand, and politics.

Iraq Invades Kuwait

Government leaders of Kuwait figured they could probably settle their dispute with Iraq peacefully, by using **diplomacy.** They believed that Saddam Hussein had placed his troops on Kuwait's border to show them just how mighty his army was.

This Kuwaiti family fled after Iraq invaded their homeland. Here, their papers are checked at the border of Jordan.

Taking over

They were wrong. At 2:00 A.M. on August 2, 1990, the Iraqi army invaded Kuwait. As the Iraqis rolled through Kuwait, they met with little resistance. A few hours after they entered the country, Iraqi tanks were barreling down the six-lane highway that led to Kuwait's capital, Kuwait City. The city's residents fled in fear, taking refuge over the border in Saudi Arabia. Soon, Iraqi helicopters began dropping bombs on Kuwait City. Then tanks and other armored vehicles entered the city, carrying about 140,000 troops who began taking over—street by street, block by block.

While the **emir** of Kuwait had been quickly **evacuated** to Saudi Arabia, many members of the royal family were still at the Dasman Palace in Kuwait City. Eventually, Iraqi soldiers made their way to the palace. The royal family put up a fight, and the emir's brother was killed.

Twelve hours after they had entered the country, the Iraqis had complete control over Kuwait, and Saddam Hussein declared that Kuwait was now a part of Iraq. With the **annexation** of Kuwait, Hussein now controlled one-fifth of the world's known oil reserves.

Threatening Saudi Arabia

After taking over Kuwait City, the Iraqi army headed for the border of Saudi Arabia. Saudi Arabia's small army could not stand up to the powerful Iraqi units. If Saddam Hussein were to take control of this oil-rich country, he would hold a **monopoly** on oil produced in the Persian Gulf. There was no question that he would use his power to control the price of oil, or even to deny oil to countries that disagreed with his policies.

Saudi Arabia is a powerful, oil-rich country with a strong alliance to the United States.

Oil

The United States imports about 30 percent of its oil from the countries of Kuwait, Saudi Arabia, and Iraq in the Persian Gulf region. Some of the countries that allied with the United States in the Gulf War, such as Japan and some European countries, import even more oil from the Persian Gulf states.

In the United States, President George H. W. Bush announced there would be economic **sanctions** against Iraq. Countries such as Great Britain, France, and Japan soon announced that they, too, were placing **embargoes** against Iraqi imports, including oil.

Building a Coalition

As President Bush spoke with heads of nations all over the world about Iraq's invasion of Kuwait, he began to build a **coalition.** He also contacted the U.S. **Ambassador** to the **United Nations** to ask them to take action against Iraq.

The UN Security Council

Only hours after the invasion, the U.S. Ambassador to the United Nations, Thomas Pickering, called for an emergency session of the UN Security Council. The Security Council has the power to authorize peace measures or take necessary action to maintain or restore peace. Pickering had little trouble persuading council members to vote to condemn Iraq's actions. By invading Kuwait, Saddam Hussein had broken the UN Charter. He had also broken international law, which is a system of law that governs the relationships between states, or nations. While it is difficult to enforce international law, most nations follow it because it is in their best interest to do so. The Security Council voted 14–0 to condemn the attack. For the first time since the **Cold War** began, the **Soviet Union** voted the same way as the U.S. Yemen, the only Arab member of the council, did not vote.

U.S. Secretary of State James Baker (right) talks with another delegate at a UN Security Council meeting.

Taking sides

The 34 countries that contributed troops or supplies such as aircraft, helicopters, ships, tanks, and other military vehicles to the Allied military coalition against Iraq were:

- Afghanistan
- Argentina
- Australia
- Bahrain
- Bangladesh
- Belgium
- Canada
- Czechoslovakia
- Denmark
- Egypt
- France
- Germany
- Greece
- Hungary
- Honduras

- Italy
- Kuwait
- Morocco
- The Netherlands
- New Zealand
- Niger
- Norway
- Oman
- Pakistan
- Poland
- Portugal
- Qatar
- Saudi Arabia
- Senegal
- South Korea

- Spain
- Syria
- Turkey
- The United Arab Emirates
- The United Kingdom
- The United States

Iraq supporters
- Jordan
- Yemen
- Libya
- Sudan
- Mauritania
- Palestine Liberation Organization

Some Arab countries were not enthusiastic about joining a coalition against Iraq. To persuade one Arab country, Egypt, to join the coalition, President Bush canceled its debt to the United States. He also granted favors to other countries that were reluctant to join.

A strong ally

In the meantime, President Bush met with Prime Minister Margaret Thatcher of the United Kingdom one of the strongest **allies** the United States had. Thatcher happened to be in the U.S. during the time of the invasion, where she was to deliver a speech. She urged Bush to take a strong stand against Saddam Hussein, and promised that Britain would side with the United States.

Soviet Union President Mikhail Gorbachev (left) sits with President Bush at the UN. Gorbachev presented a peace plan to Saddam Hussein, who rejected it, thinking that the U.S. would not engage in war.

Cheney's mission to Saudi Arabia

Then Bush called upon his Defense Secretary, Dick Cheney—who later became vice-president under Bush's son, George W. Bush—and asked him to fly to Saudi Arabia. Cheney's mission was to meet with King Fahd of Saudi Arabia and convince him to allow U.S. and other coalition troops into Saudi Arabia to defend the country against Iraq. First, Cheney had to persuade the king that Saudi Arabia was faced with an immediate threat of invasion from Iraq.

On August 6, the two men met. King Fahd listened to Cheney's proposal, and after a short discussion with his advisers, he turned to Cheney and said that he would allow coalition troops into his country. The next day, August 7, President Bush ordered the **deployment** of troops to the Persian Gulf region.

Resolution 661

Also on August 6, the UN Security Council passed a resolution calling for economic **sanctions** against Iraq. Resolution 661 called for economic sanctions including withholding **assets** Iraq had in UN member countries as well as refusing to buy from or sell anything to Iraq, except for items considered to be **humanitarian,** such as medicine or food.

Operation Desert Shield

On August 7, 1990, President Bush ordered troops to be **deployed** to the Persian Gulf region in a military buildup called Operation Desert Shield. The operation was a combined effort with Egypt and Saudi Arabia. On August 8, Great Britain announced that it was also sending troops, calling its operation GRANBY, a code name for the Gulf War.

Goals

The goals of the operation were to defend Saudi Arabia against possible invasion, remove the Iraqis from Kuwait and protect foreigners from **coalition** countries who were living in Kuwait. About 3,000 American **civilians** lived and worked in Kuwait at the time of the invasion. In addition, 3,000 British citizens, 4,000 Turkish citizens, and thousands of Indians worked at various jobs in its oil fields. When Iraq occupied Kuwait, the people who had not escaped the country became little more than hostages. They were not allowed to leave and were harassed, even tortured, by the Iraqi army as it took control of Kuwait.

This Egyptian Ranger Battalion's desert training experience helped U.S. and European troops who were unfamiliar with the dry terrain.

Transporting troops

The movement of troops and equipment was a huge undertaking. To transport the people required to carry out Operation Desert Shield, the U.S. military landed a plane in Saudi Arabia every seven minutes.

On August 22, many reserve and National Guard units were called upon to assist in Operation Desert Shield. On the same day, Navy **minesweepers** were sent to the Persian Gulf area.

On September 12, the U.S. Army contacted 500 of its retired soldiers and asked them to return to duty, the first time this had been done in the United States. By October 15, about 240,000 American troops were in the Persian Gulf region.

From the United States alone, 690,000 people, 100 naval vessels, 2,000 tanks, 1,800 fixed-wing aircraft, and 1,700 helicopters became involved in the operation. This made it the largest military undertaking since the **Vietnam War.** Aircraft carriers that were stationed in the area were ordered to the Persian Gulf, such as the USS *Independence* and the USS *Dwight D. Eisenhower* carrier battle groups. The latter was soon relieved by the USS *Saratoga.* On August 10, two hospital ships, the *Mercy* and the *Comfort*, were ordered to the Middle East.

The U.S. Aircraft Carrier Saratoga *in the Suez Canal, which runs between the Red Sea and the Mediterranean Sea in Egypt.*

Other countries that had agreed to the **sanctions** against Iraq sent troops and military equipment to the region. Along with tanks and aircraft, Britain sent about 43,000 troops, Saudi Arabia about 50,000, and Egypt about 30,200. France deployed 16,000 troops, and Syria, Oman, Qatar, and the United Arab Emirates also sent troops.

Iraq responds

Saddam Hussein reacted to the flood of coalition troops by building up his military forces in Kuwait. As Iraqi occupation of the country continued, about 336,000 Iraqi soldiers were sent to the area, along with approximately 9,000 armored vehicles.

Central Command

During the presidency of Jimmy Carter, from 1977 to 1981, the **Soviet Union** and Iran were seen as possible threats to the Middle East. Because that region was so important to the United States. President Carter developed a military arm called Rapid **Deployment** Force to oversee the area.

The origins of CENTCOM

The next president, Ronald Reagan, changed the name of the Rapid Deployment Force to United States Central Command, or CENTCOM. Its mission was to develop a plan for military action in the Persian Gulf region, as well as in Southeast Asia. In 1988, General H. Norman Schwarzkopf, who was later given the nickname "Stormin' Norman" because of his fiery temper, was named as the head of CENTCOM.

CENTCOM, which is headquartered at MacDill Air Force Base in Tampa, Florida, began to train specific units of the U.S. Army to fight in the Middle East. The first unit they named to be sent to the Middle East, if needed, was the 82nd Airborne Division. This unit, along with other selected units, such as Army Rangers, received desert training.

General Norman H. Schwarzkopf's leadership during Operations Desert Shield and Desert Storm earned him the nickname "Stormin' Norman."

The Gulf War plan

When Iraq invaded Kuwait, CENTCOM had to develop a precise military plan. It included an initial massive air assault on Iraq that would knock out communications and transportation routes, and also disable many other facilities used by the Iraqi army. When the air attack was complete, ground troops would cross into Kuwait and make their way into the central part of the country, then to Kuwait City, eventually surrounding the Iraqi army.

A great challenge for CENTCOM during the war was the coordination of the U.S.-led **coalition.** It was the largest multinational force joined to fight since World War II. CENTCOM had to make sure that its communications flowed smoothly among coalition members. This was not easy because of the various languages spoken and the different kinds of communication and military equipment used by the **allied** forces.

President Bush meets in the Oval Office with his military advisors, including, from left, Colin Powell, Dick Cheney, James Baker, and Brent Scowcroft.

Decision makers

During the Gulf War, General Schwarzkopf was named as the officer in charge of all U.S. troops, including the Air Force, Army, and Navy. Air Force Lieutenant General Charles Horner was put in charge of all U.S. and allied air force elements during the war.

Heading up the White House decision-making team, besides President Bush, were Secretary of State James Baker, Chairman of the Joint Chiefs of Staff Colin Powell, National Security Adviser Brent Scowcroft, and Secretary of Defense Dick Cheney.

The Deadline Looms

Sanctions against Iraq continued, but Saddam Hussein seemed to ignore them. The Iraqi army continued to occupy Kuwait and showed no signs of leaving. In fact, Saddam Hussein sent more Iraqi troops into Kuwait. As they watched the Iraqi troop buildup in Kuwait, **allied** military commanders changed their plans. At first they thought they would need about 250,000 soldiers to carry out Operation Desert Shield. As time passed and the Iraqi presence increased, this number went up and eventually more than doubled.

Resolution 678

On November 29, 1990, the **UN** Security Council passed Resolution 678. The resolution addressed Iraq's refusal to obey the resolution the council had passed on August 2, 1990, which demanded Iraq's immediate withdrawal from Kuwait. Resolution 678 gave Iraq "one final opportunity, as a pause of goodwill," to withdraw. The deadline for withdrawal was given as January 15, 1991. It then stated that if Iraq continued to ignore the council's demands, UN member states could "use all necessary means" to force Iraq to withdraw from Kuwait.

President George H. W. Bush delivers his State of the Union address to Congress in January 1991, outlining his plans for Iraq.

Congress votes for war

As commander in chief of the United States, the president has the power to start a war. But the Constitution states that only Congress may declare war. This can result in confusion, as it did when it became evident that the United States was preparing to launch a war against Iraq. The UN Security Council had already authorized the use of force. President Bush and military commanders were readying for war. Some people wondered why the matter had not been brought before Congress and they pressed the president to do so.

In early January 1991, a resolution titled "Authorization for Use of Military Force Against Iraq Resolution" was brought before the U.S. Senate and House of Representatives. After several days of debate, a vote was taken. In the Senate, 52 voted to approve the resolution, while 47 voted against it. In the House, 250 voted for it, and 183 were against it. Those who voted against taking military action explained that they were not prepared for another war like the one in Vietnam, in which thousands of Americans could be killed. In addition, some members of Congress opposed the idea of fighting a war that seemed to be about oil.

U.S. Air Force medical personnel conduct a drill to practice aiding soldiers in the event of a nuclear or biochemical attack. Saddam Hussein had used such weapons in the Iran-Iraq War.

Grim predictions

On television, experts argued over what would happen if the country went to war. Some members of Congress were concerned that thousands of Americans would die in the Persian Gulf. General Schwarzkopf also expressed his concerns over possible **casualties** should the United States go to war with Iraq. The Iraqi army was known to be large and powerful, and was rumored to have **chemical** and **biological weapons.** No one knew for sure whether Saddam Hussein would use these weapons.

Enforcing the embargo

As the deadline approached, the **embargo** against Iraq continued. Allied ships stopped all vessels from sailing into and out of Iraq to make sure they were not transporting goods for trade. During Operation Desert Shield, Navy personnel intercepted almost 8,000 ships, most of them in the Red Sea. Many military officers watched the embargo nervously. They believed that if there was a conflict at sea involving Iraqi and allied ships, Hussein might respond by harming **civilians** who were trapped in Kuwait.

Desert Storm Begins

The **allied coalition** brought together by President Bush had agreed that the United States would lead the way in planning military action against Iraq. American military leaders, led by General Schwarzkopf, had begun planning their strategies soon after the August 2, 1990, invasion, but hoped they would not have to use them. It soon became obvious, however, that the **sanctions** imposed on Iraq were doing little to influence Saddam Hussein to pull out of Kuwait. The enormous buildup of troops in Operation Desert Shield also seemed to have little effect on the Iraqis.

An AH-64 Apache helicopter lifts off in the desert during Operation Desert Shield. These helicopters were instrumental in destroying Iraq's key radar equipment.

The January 15 deadline passed, and it seemed as though nothing would happen. Nineteen hours after the deadline passed, however, the allied coalition's assault began. Called Operation Desert Storm, it would be the shortest and most intense war in American history.

Air power

Military planners knew that the only way to gain ground in the assault was to gain air superiority. The goal of the coalition forces was to attack Iraq from the air and destroy all its army's capabilities. The top priority was ensuring that the Iraqi military would not be able to send messages from unit to unit and to its headquarters.

The attack began at 1:00 A.M. on January 17, 1991, Baghdad time and continued for days. The first aircraft to go in were U.S. Army *AH-64 Apache* attack helicopters, which dropped bombs on radar installations. Without these installations, the Iraqi army could not track or locate coalition aircraft. F-117 aircraft, also called stealth aircraft because they are almost undetectable by radar, also flew over Iraq. They dropped bombs that destroyed command and control centers where troop movements were tracked and orders given out to the Iraqi army. These and other sites targeted in the war were located through the use of satellite imagery. Satellites in space sent pictures of Iraq to computers used by CENTCOM.

Many of the Iraqi command centers were in underground **bunkers**. But the United States had developed bombs that were powerful enough to destroy them, too. The U.S. also used what were called "smart" bombs, which are weapons that are computer-driven and are much more accurate than traditional missiles. Of the 250,000 bombs and cruise missiles dropped during the war, only a few more than 300 were smart bombs. But because they are so precise, smart bombs did 75 percent of the damage.

Other targets included surface-to-air missile sites, air-defense control sites, communications links, and air bases. The purpose of attacking these targets was to disable the Iraqi army and destroy its supplies and supply routes. Forces from the United States, Canada, Germany, Saudi Arabia, Britain, France, Italy, Bahrain, Oman, Qatar, Turkey, and the United Arab Emirates conducted bombing campaigns.

Scud missiles launched on Israel

On January 18, the Iraqis sent seven Scud missiles into Israel's capital, Tel Aviv. A close ally of the United States, Israel was not included in the coalition for political reasons. After spotting the Scud missiles heading their way, the Israeli government's first thought was to launch an attack against Iraq. However, the Bush administration had strongly urged Israel to stay out of the war. After a tension-filled day of telephone calls between Israel and the United States, Israel decided to hold off on attacking Iraq.

Scud and Patriot missiles

The kinds of Scud missiles the Iraqis used against Israel are shot from mobile launchers, which are on tractor trailers. Scuds can cause a great deal of damage to their targets. They are hard to direct, however, and often do not land precisely where intended. For the Iraqis, just landing them was probably enough. During the course of the war, it is estimated that the Iraqis launched 40 Scud missiles against Israel and 46 against Saudi Arabia. One attack on a U.S. barracks in the Saudi city of Dhahran on February 25 killed 27 Americans. To counterattack Scud missiles, the United States used Patriot missiles.

Israeli troops carefully remove a Scud missile that did not explode when it hit its target.

The Air War: Instant Thunder

Gaining air superiority was a key factor in the **allied coalition's** success in the Gulf War. The U.S. Air Force played the most important role in the war. It was able to knock out much of the Iraqi army's weapons and communications systems with bombs, guaranteeing that the Iraqis could not use those means to fight back. After only three days, much of what the allies intended to do was accomplished. The operation performed in the first days of the air assault was called "Instant Thunder." It focused on 487 targets to be hit during the air war. Of those targets, 144 were to be bombed in the first 24 hours.

Coalition forces bomb Baghdad on the night of January 25, 1991.

All together, coalition army and navy air units flew about 112,000 **sorties** against the Iraqi army. Army helicopters and other aircraft flew 30,000 more. They dropped more than 80,000 tons of bombs that destroyed 1,385 tanks and 930 other types of vehicles. They also destroyed other important targets, including facilities that allies suspected were being used to make **chemical** and **biological weapons.**

Human casualties

The bombs killed people as well. Because the accuracy of Iraqi information released after the war is questionable, it is difficult to determine exactly how many people died from the bombing. Iraq claims that some 100,000 Iraqi soldiers and about 45,000 **civilians** were killed, and thousands more were injured. The U.S. Defense Intelligence Agency estimates that the number of soldiers killed is correct, but that perhaps 3,000 Iraqi civilians were killed in the bombings.

The words of an Iraqi lieutenant

After the war, Kuwaitis searching a **bunker** that had been deserted by Iraqi troops found a diary written by an Iraqi lieutenant. Anticipating the war to come, he wrote on January 15, 1991:

We are there [Kuwait] and it is a historic right that was stolen from us when we could do nothing. The army is in a state of total alert to prepare itself against allied and American aggression expected against our well-loved territory. I am very worried for my parents because I know what these conditions represent for them. But God is good. We wish the war had not happened, but it has, so combat would be welcome.

The hole in this building shows some of the bombing damage inflicted on Iraq during the war.

Nighttime bombing raids

Many of the bombing runs were conducted at night. By flying at night, coalition forces ensured that by the time they were detected, it was too late for Iraqi soldiers to escape or to defend themselves. The nighttime raids also put fear into the hearts of the Iraqis, and this fear motivated many Iraqi soldiers to surrender.

Most coalition planes had special **sensors** that allowed the crew to see at night what was on the ground. The Iraqis had buried some of their armored vehicles under the desert sand. Heat-seeking sensors could locate these. Other aircraft had **jamming** capabilities. In other words, they had technology on board that could stop Iraqi radio transmissions and blind Iraqi radar. If they sighted an enemy aircraft, Iraqi soldiers could not use their radios to warn others, who could possibly shoot down the planes or helicopters. Because of such technology, coalition **casualties** were much fewer than had been expected.

At first, the Iraqi Air Force tried to fight back against the continual bombing. Thirty-five Iraqi aircraft were destroyed while in the air. No coalition aircraft were destroyed in this way. As the air assault continued—bombs struck the Iraqi army some 22,000 times—Iraqi troops became desperate. They parked airplanes next to holy and historic sites, knowing coalition pilots would be unwilling to bomb those places. They placed civilians at prime targets for the same reason.

Psychological warfare

Besides attacks from the air, CENTCOM also used another tactic against the Iraqi army: psychological warfare operations, called psyops, by the military. Before the war even began, psyops units of the U.S. Army were preparing leaflets to drop from the sky onto Iraqi troops. About 30 million different kinds of leaflets were distributed during the war.

One leaflet dropped was the surrender pass. U.S. Army psyops units knew that as time passed Iraqi troops became more discouraged. Psyops prepared several million leaflets that instructed Iraqi soldiers how to surrender to coalition forces. The leaflets were written in Arabic and dropped from planes onto locations where Iraqi troops were staying. When allied troops later came upon surrendering Iraqi soldiers, many of them had the leaflets in their pockets.

The Ground War

The official start date of the ground war was February 24, 1991, but several ground battles had occurred before that date. One battle took place on January 29–30, when the Iraqis entered Saudi Arabia and took control of the Saudi town of Khafji. On February 13, more fighting occurred along the Saudi border when **allies** attacked Iraqi troops lining up in what looked to be a potential invasion. Thousands of Iraqis died in air attacks during that battle—the ground war was supported from the air—and more than 1,000 were taken prisoner.

A line of coalition tanks and other assault vehicles roll into Kuwait.

Gorbachev tries to avert war

Leaders of the **Soviet Union** had made earlier attempts to **negotiate** a peaceful solution between the United States and Saddam Hussein. Hussein did not give in. Just before the official ground assault was scheduled to begin, Russia's President Gorbachev once again tried to avoid war by contacting President Bush and Saddam Hussein with a new idea for peace. The air war had been so devastating that Iraq had essentially already lost. A ground war, Gorbachev thought, would bring massive humiliation to Hussein. To avoid that, he proposed that Hussein again be given three weeks to withdraw his troops from Kuwait.

President Bush and his advisers considered the plan. The plans for the start of the ground war on February 23 were well underway. Bush decided that he would go along with Gorbachev's idea, but instead of three weeks, he would give the Iraqis one week to totally withdraw.

Some Iraqi troops had transistor radios and listened to this new plan eagerly. Iraqi soldiers who were interviewed as prisoners of war or after the war ended have said that they had hoped the Soviet plan would work, because they did not want to fight **coalition** forces. But the deadline came and went, and the Iraqis made no move to leave. Their forces were seriously weakened, though. Up to 84,000 Iraqi troops had already deserted as a result of the air strikes.

The ground war begins

The plan for the ground war was to take two approaches. The first would go straight through Iraq's defenses at the Kuwaiti border. The second approach was to go into southern Iraq, then head east toward Kuwait City. Coalition forces knew they would face 43 Iraqi divisions on the ground. Most of these soldiers were behind minefields, barbed wire, and oil-filled trenches along the Saudi-Kuwaiti border. Some of them had been there for weeks, hiding in underground **bunkers.**

Diverting Iraq's attention

At sea, thousands of coalition marines purposely drew attention to themselves by practicing for an invasion along the Kuwaiti coast. They wanted to divert Iraq's attention from the coalition assault that was to come from the Saudi border and shoreline. The Iraqi army stationed six divisions along the shoreline to prepare for the marines. One marine force played tank noises and explosion sounds over a loudspeaker so the Iraqis would think the invasion was coming at any minute.

At 4:00 A.M. on February 24, 66,000 U.S. Marines in Saudi Arabia attacked from the north into Kuwait. They crossed over dangerous mine fields and raced through Iraqi defenses. When the Iraqi soldiers saw how easily the marines crossed over their lines, about 800 of them crawled out of their bunkers and surrendered. At the same time, Saudi and other Arab forces went up along the Kuwaiti coast.

Later that day, British, French, and American forces began the second approach, entering Kuwait, then splitting up, with some going east and the rest heading north. Mostly French forces remained in the west, while most of the British and American forces went toward Kuwait City. Their pace was slowed by mass surrenders of Iraqi soldiers. Instead of fighting back, the soldiers laid down their guns and raised their hands.

Friendly fire

In wartime, it is not unusual for one side to accidentally kill its own troops. This is called friendly fire. During the Gulf War, 65 American soldiers—almost half of all U.S. troops killed in the war—were killed by friendly fire. Nine British soldiers were killed in one friendly fire incident when a U.S. pilot, thinking they were Iraqis, dropped a bomb on their vehicle. Military experts view friendly fire as an inevitable part of war but are constantly working to find ways to reduce it.

Iraqi soldiers waved whatever white fabric they could find to signal their surrender to coalition forces.

Technology

Here, a F-117 stealth bomber refuels. These planes earned the nickname "wobbly goblins" because they wobble when they fly.

One reason the **allied coalition** was able to gain superiority during the Gulf War was because it had access to the latest weapons, communications, and detections systems. The Iraqi army was using outdated technology from the 1980s.

Global Positioning System

In the desert, everything looks the same. There are no landmarks, just sand as far as the eye can see. There are no landmarks to help tell north from south and east from west. During Operation Desert Storm, allied soldiers used the **Global Positioning System** (GPS). They used GPS receivers to pinpoint their location and to plot their moves. It was the first time this technology was used in a war.

GPS uses 24 satellites that broadcast signals indicating their position in space. GPS receivers pick up the signals from three of these satellites to determine their location. The use of GPS gave the allies an advantage over the Iraqis, who did not have them. Iraqi soldiers often got lost in the desert.

Aircraft

The coalition used several different kinds of airplanes in the war. One kind looks much like a commercial jet on the outside, because it uses a Boeing 707 frame. The difference is that this airplane has a large, rotating disk on the top called a radome. The aircraft carry the Airborne Warning and Control System, so they are called AWACS. They have the ability to jam radio signals, guide bombers to their targets, and act as command posts for other aircraft.

The B-52 Stratofortress is a large airplane that can carry up to 60,000 lbs (27,216 kg) of bombs. It also carries machine guns or cannons in its tail that are used to shoot down other planes. In Operation Desert Storm, B-52s were used for "carpet" bomb attacks, meaning they dropped many bombs over a large area.

The F-117 stealth fighter was also used during Operation Desert Storm. The aircraft was developed to avoid radar detection and is shaped like a bat. During the war, F-117s were able to fly into Iraq without being seen by radar, so their bombing attacks were a surprise. Only one person can sit inside an F-117. During the Gulf War, they were most often used to destroy Iraqi control-and-command centers.

The main attack helicopter used by the U.S. Army during Operation Desert Storm was the AH-64 Apache Attack helicopter. The primary targets of Apaches were tanks and fighting vehicles. Each Apache has a pilot night vision system, a radar **jammer,** and other technology necessary to complete a mission. The body of an Apache helicopter is made from substances so strong that it can be hit with rounds of ammunition and not be damaged. Apaches carried Hellfire missiles which have **sensors** in their noses that guide the missile to a **laser beam** the pilot has directed onto the target.

Warthogs

One type of warplane, the A-10, used rounds of ammunition that contained **depleted uranium.** The bullets can pierce armored metal because the substance in the bullets is very dense and burns when it strikes a target. However, depleted uranium is **radioactive,** and its use was very controversial. Today, some scientists believe that the radioactivity released by the weapons has caused high rates of cancer and other medical problems in Iraq.

One special kind of aircraft used during the war was the drone, or remotely piloted vehicle (RPV). These small planes can fly up to 100 mi (160 km) per hour and stay in the air for five hours. They are controlled by an operator on the ground using a box with a joystick. Drones act as spy planes, taking pictures and transmitting them. During the Gulf War, the pictures were sent back to battleships, which then aimed their guns at targets based on this information.

Naval weapons

Sorties were carried out from U.S. Navy aircraft carriers, and battleships launched missiles into Iraq. One kind of missile was the Tomahawk. This cruise missile shoots from a ship or a submarine and contains a guidance system that directs it to its target. Tomahawks can move up to 550 mi (885 km) an hour and are 20 ft (6 m) long. During Operation Desert Storm, 297 Tomahawk missiles were fired.

Tomahawks, such as this one being launched from the USS Mississippi, can move up to 550 mi (885 km) an hour and are 20 ft (6 m) long.

Media Coverage

Media coverage of the Gulf War was vast, or seemed so to television viewers. In truth, much of what was released was done so only after approval by the U.S. government.

Cleared by Iraqi Censors
Peter Arnett
Baghdad, Iraq
CNN LIVE

Peter Arnett, a CNN reporter, broadcasts from Baghdad during the Gulf War. The content of his report was reviewed by U.S. officials.

On the frontline

Peter Arnett, one of the CNN correspondents in Baghdad, said this about the experience of viewing the bombing firsthand:

The most frightening moment was during the first hour of the bombing when the very high-powered American explosives destroyed office towers just a few blocks away from our hotel. The impact of the explosion and the heat swept through the open windows of our hotel room. Incidents like this prompted Bernard Shaw to comment on the air: "It feels like the center of hell." It was nerve-wracking to remain in the room, but what motivated us to continue was the opportunity to talk to a worldwide audience about what we could see.

Live broadcasts

The first shots fired in Operation Desert Storm were shown live on television. Three reporters from the Cable News Network (CNN), Bernard Shaw, Peter Arnett, and John Holliman, and camera operator Mark Biello were staying on the ninth floor of the Al-Rashid Hotel in Baghdad, planning to cover the war. At 2:30 A.M. they heard bombs and antiaircraft guns. The camera operator set up three cameras on tripods—three-legged stands—and focused them on the hotel window while the reporters ducked under tables. He also held another camera, which was later taken from him by Iraqi security soldiers in the hotel.

As the bombs dropped, the reporters explained what they were hearing. Sometimes, one of them would get up and look out the window, then take cover under the table again. The broadcast was beamed by satellites for seventeen hours until the reporters in Baghdad lost power. For the first time, millions of viewers around the world saw military action at the same time military leaders and governments were seeing it.

Controlling the media

But while the initial hours of the war were shown live on television, most of the information released was **censored.** During the **Vietnam War,** news broadcasts showed images of dead and wounded soldiers on both sides. The pictures disturbed the American public, who expressed growing concern about the length of the war and the number of U.S. soldiers who were being killed. The government had learned its lesson in Vietnam, and was not about to broadcast film of dead and dying American or Iraqi soldiers.

Joint Chiefs of Staff Chairman Colin Powell briefs the press on the latest developments in the Gulf War.

Before news copy was released to the public, reporters who were stationed in Saudi Arabia had to submit it to government representatives there for what was called a security review. This included film and photographs. Later, television networks were criticized for not presenting an accurate view of what was happening in the war. Some critics also claimed that corporate sponsors and owners of television networks did not want to show unpleasant footage because it would give the networks a bad name or cause ratings to go down.

Citizens for a Free Kuwait

Even before the war started, a group called Citizens for a Free Kuwait used the media to spread its message. The group hired a public relations company to spread information about what was happening in Kuwait. In October 1990, a person the company hired went before a member of Congress and told them about the horrors done by Iraqi soldiers in a Kuwaiti hospital. Later, it was discovered that the story was not true and that Citizens for a Free Kuwait was paid by the Kuwaiti government to try to get U.S. backing for the war by gaining the sympathy of the American people.

Press briefings

The government also controlled information by giving televised press briefings, which were meetings for the press during which they described the progress of the war and showed video of targets being damaged. During the briefings, military representatives used language that many claimed clouded or covered up the real damage being done. For example, to describe the fact that innocent Iraqi **civilians** were killed during a bombing, they would use the term "collateral damage."

The Home Front

Most Americans supported the war with Iraq. In fact, on January 16, 1991, the day after the **UN** Security Council deadline, a poll showed that 76 percent of Americans approved of going to war with Iraq.

Recession

One reason the American public wanted to go to war was that the country at the time was in a **recession.** History has shown that wars create jobs. Because the equipment used in a war is quickly depleted and must continually be replaced, more people are need to work. People felt that if there was a war, there would be more jobs. New jobs meant that more people would spend money, which would strengthen the economy.

Ribbons and T-shirts

One way Americans showed support to troops during the war was by displaying yellow ribbons. In recent years, yellow ribbons had become a symbol for remembrance. When someone went away, loved ones left behind tied a yellow ribbon around a tree or a fence post until he or she returned. During the Persian Gulf War, yellow ribbons appeared all over the country. People not only tied them around flags, trees, fences, and signs, but also began wearing them on their shirts and jackets.

Desert Storm T-shirts and other items also became popular during the war. To show their support, people bought and wore T-shirts decorated with eagles and helicopters flying over a desert. Americans wore Desert Storm baseball caps, drank their coffee from Desert Storm mugs, and drove cars with Desert Storm bumper stickers and license plates.

The American people showed their support for the Persian Gulf War by decorating everyday objects with yellow ribbon and patriotic colors.

Letters

Schoolchildren also got behind the effort, writing thousands of letters to soldiers stationed in the Persian Gulf region. U.S. Marine Lieutenant Colonel Ted Herman said that, "Support from home was wonderful, they kept sending us tapes, books, and letters, and we all made friends with school kids through the mail. I had a 4th grade class I'd write to.... The kids would send me pictures of themselves and ask what it was like being shot at and so on."

Antiwar protests

If polls and demonstrations were any indication, those who did not support the war were in the minority. During the **Vietnam War**, thousands of Americans protested, and the number against the war grew as the war continued year after year. But the Persian Gulf War was over in a matter of weeks, which may have been why there were so few protests. Of the protests that did occur, perhaps the largest was held in January in Washington, D.C. Thousands of people from all over the country gathered to protest the Persian Gulf War. Other cities, such as Seattle, Washington, were also the site of protests. Antiwar activists shouted slogans such as, "No blood for oil" and "**cease-fire** now."

Approval rating

At the end of the war, President Bush's approval rating—the public's opinion of how the president is doing their job—was 90 percent, the highest it had ever been. This meant that 90 percent of the people questioned said they approved of how Bush had handled the war.

The People Suffer

Many Kuwaiti and Iraqi people suffered during the war. In Kuwait, those who had not escaped were subject to mistreatment by the Iraqi army. In Iraq, **coalition** bombing killed many **civilians** and knocked out power and water facilities.

The Kuwaitis

During its 7-month occupation of Kuwait, the Iraqi army mistreated, tortured, and killed many people of Kuwait. At least 1,000 Kuwaitis were murdered, and people from other countries who lived in Kuwait. The actions of the

*The **emir**'s palace in Kuwait City was destroyed by the Iraqi Army.*

Iraqis were war crimes. As news of the abuses was revealed after the war, governments around the world called for Saddam Hussein to be put on trial to answer for his actions and those of his troops.

Iraqi troops removed residents from their homes and sent them to detention centers. Investigators who later toured the country discovered at least 24 sites where horrible tortures were carried out.

People who remained in their homes lived in constant fear that **chemical** and **biological weapons** would be used against them. Rumors of the deadly Iraqi weapons had been around for years. During the occupation, Kuwaiti scientists continually tested the public water supply to see if it had been poisoned.

Most medical services in Kuwait were shut down during the occupation. The nation's water treatment system was neglected and soon unable to work. This resulted in the Kuwaitis having to pump raw sewage into the Persian Gulf.

Iraqi soldiers also looted Kuwait, taking anything they could find. Equipment from businesses, hospitals, and schools was stolen and sent to Iraq. Cars and trucks were stolen and taken for joy rides or driven to Iraq. Private homes of people who had fled the country—many of them non-Kuwaiti citizens who were there to work—were looted, their valuables gone forever.

Thousands of people, especially those who were not Kuwaiti citizens, fled the country as Iraq invaded. During Iraq's occupation of Kuwait, more than a half-million Kuwaitis went into **exile.** A large number of those who remained were taken hostage and moved to Iraq. More than 4,000 of them were British citizens. In 2002, more than 600 Kuwaiti hostages still had not been released, and their whereabouts are unknown.

The Iraqis

The people of Iraq also suffered greatly during the Gulf War. Air raids destroyed electrical power plants, including those that supplied hospitals, so what medical care the people could get was hindered by lack of electricity. According to U.S. military leaders, after **allied** warplanes bombed some of Baghdad's electrical power plants, Saddam Hussein ordered the rest be turned off. The lack of electricity also affected sewage treatment and water treatment plants. There was not enough clean water to go around.

Many Iraqis suffered from illness and starvation as a result of the war. These Iraqi children are searching for food in a garbage dump in Saddam City, Iraq.

By the middle of January 1991, after days of bomb attacks, many people in Iraq were forced to drink water from the Tigris River. They also washed clothes and kitchen utensils in water supplies that had been contaminated by raw sewage. Because the sewage plants were not working, raw sewage was being pumped into the river and sometimes flowed into the streets.

Because coalition air forces had bombed as many communications headquarters as they could find, telephone and mail services also went down during the war. The main bridges and highways in the country were also destroyed by bombs; many people could not get to medical help. Even after the **cease-fire**, Iraq had great difficulty trying to find parts to fix destroyed buildings, bridges, and highways. Because of the **embargo**, it could not import parts it needed to fix them.

Victory

On February 25, Saddam Hussein ordered his army to withdraw from Kuwait. Most of the Iraqi army, however, was trapped by the **allies**, who were closing in on all sides. On February 26, the first Arab forces made their way into Kuwait City. That same day, U.S. Marines had taken over Kuwait City International Airport.

The highway of death

The Iraqis began to attempt to escape, realizing they were defeated. About 40,000 Iraqi soldiers fled Kuwait City, many of them in cars and trucks they had stolen from **exiled** Kuwaitis. The vehicles were filled with objects the Iraqis had stolen from abandoned Kuwaiti homes. The only way out of Kuwait City was the same six-lane highway they had used to enter it with their tanks and armored trucks. As the Iraqis drove down the highway with their stolen goods, **coalition** aircraft fired on them. At least 4,000 vehicles and countless bodies lay scattered over what is now known as the highway of death.

This U.S. Special Forces soldier (with weapon) is thanked by a crowd of grateful Kuwaitis.

Kuwait liberated

At 8:00 A.M. on February 28, the war was declared over, and a **cease-fire** was put into effect. When U.S. marines entered Kuwait City, its members, who had heard that most residents had fled, were surprised to see the streets filled with cheering Kuwaitis. People waved flags from rooftops and were filled with joy.

Except for those who attempted to travel on the highway of death, the surviving members of the Iraqi army were able to flee Kuwait. Later, military leaders were criticized for allowing this to happen. Many military analysts believed it would have been better to destroy the army completely. President George H. W. Bush has stated that he stopped the war when he did because his military commanders told him that the mission was complete—the Iraqi army had pulled out of Kuwait. If coalition forces had gone into Baghdad with the intention of overthrowing the Iraqi government, many more American soldiers would have been killed. In addition, the U.S. government would then have had to occupy Iraq, in essence remaining there indefinitely. And while U.S. allies agreed with the goals of the Gulf War, they did not support the idea of overthrowing the government of Iraq.

General Schwarzkopf speaks to an Iraqi officer through an interpreter about conditions of the cease-fire.

Cease-fire

On March 3, General Schwarzkopf, along with the Saudi commander of the Joint Arab/**Islamic** Force and other coalition commanders, met with Iraqi generals at the Iraqi city of Safwan to **negotiate** details of the cease-fire. On April 7, 1991, Iraq officially accepted the terms of the cease-fire, including allowing a **UN** weapons inspections team to enter the country periodically and make sure it was not producing nuclear, **chemical,** or **biological weapons.**

At the end of the war, the 85,000 prisoners of war (POWs) held by the allied coalition were released. The Iraqis released a small number of allied POWs on March 4, and the majority of prisoners on March 5. Fewer than 50 allied troops were made prisoners of war.

The fighting in the Persian Gulf War was over quickly, and fewer Americans were killed than anyone predicted. President George H. W. Bush, his cabinet, and his advisers, were applauded for their part in the victory. General H. Norman Schwarzkopf was regarded as a hero, as were the hundreds of thousands of American military personnel who took part in the war.

On June 8, 1991, a victory parade was held in Washington, D.C. Nearly one million people attended the parade. General Schwarzkopf and his staff led the parade. The officers and 9,000 U.S. troops marched. Eighty-three military aircraft flew overhead.

Women in the Gulf War

More than 40,000 women served in the Gulf War. This was more than had served in any previous war. Sixteen women were killed in the war, and two were taken prisoner. While women served in many support roles in the war, including flying aircraft, military law prohibited them from combat missions. As soon as the war ended, though, Colorado Representative Pat Schroeder sponsored a bill that would allow women to fly in combat. The bill passed in 1994, and now about 100 women are eligible to fly in combat situations.

Environmental Disaster in Kuwait

Oil well fires rage outside Kuwait City in the aftermath of the war. The Iraqis set fire to the wells before they left Kuwait.

Before the Iraqis fled, they exploded about 92 percent of the oil wells in Kuwait. Oil gushed out of the wells, and some wells immediately caught fire from the explosions. Beginning in January 1991, Iraqi troops also released crude oil into the Persian Gulf. The oil released from the oil spills and damaged oil wells caused an environmental catastrophe. About eleven million barrels of crude oil a day were lost, for a total of 1.5 billion barrels of oil. The loss cost Kuwait tens of thousands of dollars every hour.

The exploded oil wells caught fire and continued to burn for weeks, some even for months. The Kuwait Oil Company hired firefighters from around the world, but primarily the United States, to fight the fires. At first it seemed like an impossible job. The fires covered vast expanses of land, and temperatures reached 2,000°F (1,093°C). Flames shot as high as 200 feet (61 meters) into the air, and desert winds blew the smoke for miles. The air was so thick with smoke that at times firefighters could barely see their hand in front of their face.

Land mines

Before they fled Kuwait, Iraqi troops planted more than half a million land mines along its borders, including along the shoreline. As a term of **cease-fire,** Iraq revealed where it had planted the mines. Still, in the first year following the Gulf War, 1,300 Kuwaiti people were killed or wounded after coming across land mines. Fifty of the bomb-removal specialists called in to remove the mines were killed when mines exploded.

Other explosives also littered the Kuwaiti landscape. Iraqi soldiers left behind tons of unexploded bombs and ammunition. About one-third of the 100,000 tons (9,072 metric tons) of explosives **coalition** forces dropped on Kuwait did not explode when they hit the soft desert sand. As time passed, winds covered some of these explosives. Any vehicle that drove over them could be blown up.

As the wells burned, the escaping oil slowly seeped into the sandy soil of Kuwait and ran along the ground in rivers. In low places, the rivers of oil gathered into lakes. Birds, mistaking the oil lakes for water, landed, became stuck, and died.

One island in the Persian Gulf, Karan Island, was a breeding ground for rare green sea turtles. Before breeding season began, a cleanup company worked for days to remove oily sand from the island to inland sand pits. Sand dug from pits was then put on the island's shores so the turtles would have clean sand in which to bury their eggs.

Smoke and destruction

Burning crude oil produced smoke that blanketed Kuwait for months. Everyone breathed in the thick, oily smoke. It coated their skin, their clothes, and the outside of their homes. No one was certain what kind of physical, long-term effects this would have.

Because the smoke was so thick, it kept the sun's rays from reaching the Persian Gulf. As a result, the top layer of the gulf cooled down. These cooler temperatures had an effect on marine life that had adapted to warmer temperatures. In shallow water especially, most marine life disappeared for a few months, probably to find warmer water.

An oil-covered duck suffers from the aftermath of the Gulf War. In the background, smoke plumes from a burning oil well rise into the sky.

Besides damage from released crude oil, the desert surface was damaged as heavy tanks and other vehicles drove across it. The top layer of sand was torn up, releasing the finer sand underneath. As a result, there are now more sandstorms in Kuwait, and the country has about 1,300 more sand dunes than it did before the war. The damage from the vehicles destroyed plants, although most of them grew back after several months.

Kuwait and Iraq After the War

After the war ended, Kuwait and Iraq began to rebuild. Although most of the damage in Kuwait—except for environmental damage—was repaired by 1992, many people in Iraq continued to suffer from the effects of the war long after it ended.

Saddam Hussein lived in several luxurious homes in Iraq. By the end of 1992, Saddam Hussein had rebuilt his palace in Baghdad.

Kuwait rebuilds

By 1992, oil production in Kuwait rose to the level it had been before the war. The water treatment system was working. The country also began to rebuild its defense system, ordering tanks and other war equipment. In 2000, the **UN** Compensation Commission awarded **reparations** totaling $15.9 million to a Kuwaiti oil company for losses it suffered.

Rebuilding Iraq

By April 1991, serious diseases such as **cholera** and **typhoid** had spread throughout Iraq, brought about by lack of fresh water and proper sewage facilities. Many people, mostly children, died. Medical staff could do little to help the sick because hospitals had no running water and no power.

Sanctions and frozen overseas **assets** resulted in a severe food shortage in Iraq. By August of 1991, about 11,000 Iraqis had starved to death. By November 1991, there were food riots all around Iraq as starving Iraqis clamored to feed their families. After hearing about the suffering of the Iraqi people, the sanctions committee of the UN Security Council agreed to release Iraq's assets in 31 countries to buy food and medicine.

Around Baghdad, facilities were rebuilt fairly quickly. By October 1992, the telephone system and all but one of the bridges in Baghdad had been repaired. Power stations were also being rebuilt, and some were operating by that time.

The Shi'ites and the Kurds

Immediately after the Gulf War, Saddam Hussein turned against two groups in his own country. On March 8, 1991, soon after the war ended, the Iraqi army attacked the **Shi'ite** town of Karbala from the air. The Shi'ite people in southern Iraq had been oppressed by the Hussein **regime** for years, and often rebelled against the Iraqi government. At first the Shi'ites tried to fight back, but soon thousands of them fled south to take refuge in Saudi Arabia.

In the refugee camps, the Shi'ites expressed disappointment, even shock, at the refusal of the United States to help them in their struggle against Saddam Hussein. One reason the United States gave for not assisting them was that the Shi'ites in Iran were an intensely anti-American group, and they did not want to help a similar group in Iraq. Saudi Arabian leaders tried to convince the U.S. government that the Iraqi Shi'ites were not like those in Iran. In 1992, after the Shi'ite rebellion had been put down and many people were killed, President Bush decided to enforce a no-fly zone over southern Iraq.

This Kurdish family finds safety in a refugee camp. Over one million Kurds went to the mountains, or to neighboring countries Turkey and Iran to flee Hussein.

Once the Shi'ites were overcome, the Iraqi government turned to the **Kurds** in northern Iraq. Like the Shi'ites, the Kurds had been persecuted under Saddam Hussein and had tried to fight back. Realizing what Hussein could do, this time the United States stepped in, establishing protected areas in northern Iraq for the Kurds.

After the attack against Karbala, the Shi'ite people in southern Iraq were ignored. Children starved because there was not enough food, and electrical power plants still did not work. Because sewage plant pumps needed electricity to run, raw sewage flowed through the streets of Shi'ite settlements long after the streets of Baghdad had been restored to their previous condition.

Some people believe that Saddam Hussein intentionally ignored the Shi'ites because they had spoken out against him. Others wonder if by forcing the Shi'ites to live in such miserable conditions, Hussein was hoping the rest of world would feel so bad for them that it would push to have the economic sanctions lifted.

Impact of the War

Gulf War Syndrome

By about 1994, nearly 3,000 Gulf War veterans were found to have illnesses and symptoms that could not be explained. By 1995, the number had risen to 63,000, and by 2001, some 100,000 Gulf War veterans had illnesses doctors couldn't explain. **Civilians** who were involved in the war have become sick as well. The Iraqi people and former Iraqi soldiers also have similar complaints. Their symptoms vary, but include cancer, fatigue, memory loss, nervous system disorders, joint and muscle pain, breathing problems, and intestinal problems. Because no one illness seemed to explain most of the symptoms, the medical community began calling the problem Gulf War Syndrome.

The U.S. government as well as several independent organizations have studied Gulf War Syndrome, and most of them have not been able to find a connection between Gulf War factors and the illness. Still, many people believe that the illness was caused by something that occurred during the war. Some possible causes include the medicines and vaccines they were given before they went to the Persian Gulf, inhaling smoke from oil fires, and exposure to **depleted uranium** from weapons used by warthogs. Many former soldiers also believe that Saddam Hussein somehow used chemical or biological weapons against **coalition** soldiers, and that their illnesses are caused by exposure to these weapons. The medical community continues to study Gulf War Syndrome.After the war, the **UN** Special Commission (UNSCOM) appointed a team of people from countries around the world to inspect sites in Iraq where weapons are made or stored. The team visited Iraq

Scott Ritter (center), the lead inspector for UNSCOM for 7 years, resigned in 1998 because he felt hindered by Hussein's lack of cooperation in removing weapons.

regularly to make sure the country was not producing nuclear, **chemical,** or **biological weapons.**

Weapons Inspections

After the inspections program began in 1991, disagreements arose between Saddam Hussein and the UN. Hussein often refused to allow the inspectors to visit certain facilities, raising suspicions that the country was developing weapons there. At other times, the inspectors' visits were delayed, leading them to wonder if evidence had been removed from the sites before they got there. In October 1997, Hussein refused to allow some members of the inspection to enter Iraq because they were from the United States. In September 1998, the Iraqi parliament ended all cooperation with UNSCOM. In response, on December 16, 1998, the United States and Great Britain bombed suspected weapons factories in Iraq after that country refused to go along with UNSCOM's request to tour those sites.

Saddam Hussein remained in power in Iraq after the Gulf War ended.

In the following years, Saddam Hussein made no effort to comply with the terms of the cease-fire agreement. In late 2002, the administration of President George W. Bush, the son of former President George H. W. Bush, was convinced that Hussein was continuing to hide weapons from inspectors. In response to a new resolution from the UN Security Council, the UN weapons inspection team resumed inspections in Iraq. Hussein complied but with little cooperation. President George W. Bush attempted to gain support from other UN member countries to overthrow of Saddam's regime through force. Many nations, however, would not agree to support the overthrow without solid evidence that Saddam's government was a real and immediate threat to the world.

Gulf War Timeline

1990

July 17	Saddam Hussein makes speech in which he says that he will invade Kuwait unless certain demands are met
July 20	30,000 Iraqi troops are outside the Kuwaiti border
July 30	100,000 Iraqi troops, plus tanks and other equipment, are massed on the Kuwaiti border
August 2	Iraqi troops invade Kuwait at 1:00 A.M.; President Bush freezes Iraqi and Kuwaiti **assets** in the United States; **UN** Security Council votes to condemn the invasion and order Iraq to withdraw
August 3	U.S. Navy forces **deployed** to Persian Gulf
August 4	U.S. political and military leaders discuss plans for war
August 6	Cheney and Schwarzkopf travel to Saudi Arabia to meet with King Fahd, who agrees to allow U.S. troops into his country
August 8	U.S. troops begin arriving in Saudi Arabia
August 20	U.S. Army divisions begin to arrive in Saudi Arabia
August 28	Iraq annexes Kuwait
November 8	President Bush announces that about 200,000 additional forces will be sent to Persian Gulf
November 20	Members of House of Representatives file suit in Washington demanding that Bush not attack Iraq until Congress approves
November 29	UN Security Council authorizes use of force against Iraq

1991

January 9	U.S. Secretary of State James Baker goes to Geneva, Switzerland, to meet with Iraqi Foreign Minister Tariq Aziz to talk about resolving the problem
January 10	U.S. House of Representatives and Senate begin debating possible war
January 12	House and Senate approve military action
January 15	Deadline for Iraqi troops to withdraw from Kuwait passes; Iraqi troops still occupy Kuwait
January 17	Operation Desert Storm begins at 3:00 A.M. with massive air assault
January 18	Iraq launches Scud missiles against Israel
February 6	U.S. troops now number 506,000; other **coalition** troops reach 200,000
February 21	White House sets February 23 deadline for Iraqi withdrawal
February 24	Ground war begins
February 26	Iraqis flee Kuwait City
February 27	President Bush and advisers decide war is over
February 28	**Cease-fire** goes into effect at 8:00 A.M.
March 3	Schwarzkopf meets with Iraqi generals at Safwan
March 5	Most prisoners of war released
June 8	Victory parade in Washington, D.C.

Further Reading

Nonfiction

Corzine, Phyllis. *Modern Nations of the World: Iraq.* San Diego, Cal.: Lucent Books 2003.

Foster, Leila Merrill. *Enchantment of the World: Kuwait.* Danbury, Conn.: Children's Press, 1998.

Godden, John, ed. *Shield & Storm: Personal Recollections of the Air War in the Gulf.* London, Engl.: Brassey's, 1994.

Wilkinson, Philip. *Eyewitness: Islam.* New York, NY: Dorling Kindersley, 2002.

Website

PBS Frontline: The Persian Gulf War: An In-Depth Examination
http://www.pbs.org/wgbh/pages/frontline/gulf/

Glossary

allies countries who work together for a common purpose

ambassador official representative of a country, often sent to another country on an assignment

annexation the attachment of one thing to another

asset property belonging to a person, business, or country, including money, stocks, bonds, real estate, and material goods

Ba'ath party Arab political party in Syria and Iraq

biological weapon germs released into air, water, or food during wartime to make people sick or kill them

bunkers heavily protected fighting positions

casualty persons killed, wounded, missing or taken prisoner, usually during wartime

cease-fire military order to end the firing of weapons

censor take out objectionable information

chemical weapon made of substances that burn or poison humans and animals, usually gas or liquid chemicals

cholera intestinal disease caused by bacteria

civilian person not on active duty with the military

coalition union of members who work together to do something

Cold War period of hostility and tension between the United States and the Soviet Union during 1945–1991 that fell short of use of military force

depleted uranium radioactive waste product that comes from the way uranium is processed for use in atomic weapons and nuclear power plants; uranium is a radioactive element that occurs naturally in the earth

deploy send soldiers to a military base

diplomacy skillfulness at handling interaction between people or countries

embargo legal ban on importing and exporting goods

emir ruler of an Islamic country

evacuate move to a place of safety

exile a person in the state of being forced from their country or their home

fundamentalist one who strictly follows the beliefs of a particular religion or set of rules

humanitarian for the good of people

Global Positioning System (GPS) a system in space that can determine an object's position and speed on Earth

Islamic of the Muslim, or Islam, faith. Muslims, or Islamics, believe that Allah is god and Muhammad was his prophet

jammer device that stops radio waves from transmitting and stops radar from locating a target

Kurds Middle Eastern people who make their living farming and raising livestock

laser beam special kind of light beam

minesweeper ship designed to find and remove mines (explosive devices) from the sea

monopoly when one group or company controls a product or market

Muslim follower of Islam

Nazi German political party established by Adolf Hitler in the early 1930s

negotiate work out a problem between two parties

Ottoman Empire Turkish empire founded by Osman I in the late 13th century C.E.

purge removal of people who are considered disloyal or troublemakers

radioactive substance that gives off energetic particles. Radioactive elements have been proven to cause cancer and other serious illnesses, even death.

recession period of time in a country's economy when buying and selling slows down

regime form of government

reparation payment for damage done, often during a war

sanction measure used against a country that has broken international law

sensor device that detects something

Shi'ite Muslim group that believes in the teachings of the Shia form of the Islamic religion

sortie aerial mission or aerial attack

Soviet Union name of union of states in former Russia after the Revolution of 1917; also called the Union of Soviet Socialist Republics (U.S.S.R.)

superpower name for the United States and the Soviet Union, who emerged from World War II as the most powerful countries in the world

treaty agreement between countries

typhoid contagious disease caused by bacteria

United Nations (UN) association of countries formed after World War II to work for world peace

uranium radioactive substance found naturally in the earth

Vietnam War fought from 1962 to 1975 between North Vietnam and South Vietnam in Southeast Asia. North Vietnam was a communist country and tried to take over South Vietnam; the United States entered the war in defense of South Vietnam, but eventually North Vietnam won.

Index